Name _____ Class _____ Date _____ ☞ **W9-BZV-501**

Skills Worksheet

Concept Review

Section: Carbohydrates and Lipids

Complete each statement below by choosing a term from the following list. Terms may be used more than once.

carbohydrate	monosaccharide	disaccharide	polysaccharide
condensation	hydrolysis	lipid	sugar
glycogen	polymer	starch	cellulose

1. A _____ is a simple sugar that is the basic sub-unit of a carbohydrate.

2. A _____ is a carbohydrate made up of long chains of simple sugars.

3. A _____ is an organic compound made of carbon, hydrogen, and oxygen that provides nutrients to the cells of living things.

4. A _____, such as a fat or steroid, does not dissolve in water.

5. The polysaccharide that plants use for storing energy is _____.

6. A _____ is a sugar formed from two monosaccharides.

7. Many animals use an energy-storage carbohydrate called _____.

8. The carbohydrate _____ comes from wood fiber and is the most abundant organic compound on Earth.

9. A monosaccharide and a disaccharide are both examples of a simple

_____.

10. A polysaccharide or other large, chainlike molecule found in living things is

called a biological _____.

11. A _____ reaction is one in which two or more molecules combine, producing water or another simple molecule in the process.

12. A _____ reaction is one in which the decomposition of a biological polymer takes place along with the breakdown of a water molecule.

13. Many monosaccharides or disaccharides can combine to form a long chain

called a _____.

14. Maltose and sucrose are both examples of a _____.

15. Fructose and glucose are examples of a _____.

| Concept Review *continued*

16. Chitin is a _____.

17. Complete the table below.

Carbohydrate name	Structure	Role
starch		
glycogen	polysaccharide	energy storage in animals
cellulose		
sucrose	disaccharide	table sugar
glucose		
fructose	monosaccharide	sugar found in fruits
lactose		
maltose		
chitin		
amylose		

Answer the following items in the space provided.

18. Relate the structure of carbohydrates to their role in biological systems.

_____

_____

_____

_____

_____

19. What is a condensation reaction?

_____

_____

_____

_____

20. What is a hydrolysis reaction?

_____

_____

_____

_____

Name _____ Class _____ Date _____

Concept Review

Section: Proteins

Complete each statement below by choosing a term from the following list. Terms may be used more than once.

protein	amino acid	polypeptide	enzyme
denature	disulfide	primary	secondary
tertiary	quaternary	pleated sheet	helix
active site	substrate	trypsin	peptide

1. A(n) _____ is any one of twenty organic molecules that contain a carboxyl and an amino group and that combine to form proteins.

2. A(n) _____ is an organic compound made up of one or more chains of amino acids that is a principal component of all cells.

3. A(n) _____ bond is one that forms between the carboxyl group of one amino acid and the amino group of another amino acid.

4. A(n) _____ bridge can form a looped protein or two separate polypeptides.

5. Coils and folds that are often held in place by hydrogen bonds give a protein its _____ structure.

6. The three-dimensional shape of a protein is its _____ structure.

7. The amino-acid sequence of a polypeptide chain is the _____ structure of a protein.

8. A(n) _____ structure arises when different polypeptide chains that have their own three-dimensional structure come together to form a larger protein.

9. A secondary structure called an alpha- _____ is shaped like a coil with hydrogen bonds that form along a single segment of a peptide.

10. A secondary structure called a beta- _____ is shaped like an accordion with hydrogen bonds that form between adjacent polypeptide segments.

11. Because of a difference in only one _____, the entire shape of hemoglobin is different in the blood cells of people with sickle cell anemia.

12. A(n) _____ is a type of protein that speeds up metabolic reactions in plants and animals without being permanently changed or destroyed.

Name _____ Class _____ Date _____

Concept Review *continued*

13. Only a small part of an enzyme's surface, called the _____, makes an enzyme active.

14. Curly hair is the result of _____ bridges in hair proteins.

15. In reactions that use an enzyme, the reactant is called a(n) _____.

16. To cause a protein to lose its tertiary and quaternary structures is to

    _____ it.

17. A protein-splitting enzyme called _____ is used in the small intestine to help break down proteins into amino acids through hydrolysis.

Complete each item below in the space provided.

18. Describe how amino acids form proteins through condensation reactions.

    _____

    _____

    _____

    _____

    _____

19. Describe four different kinds of interactions between side chains on a polypeptide molecule that help to make the shape that a protein takes.

    _____

    _____

    _____

    _____

    _____

20. How do enzymes work?

    _____

    _____

    _____

    _____

    _____

Name _____ Class _____ Date _____

Concept Review

Section: Nucleic Acids

Complete each statement below by choosing a term from the following list. Terms may be used more than once.

nucleic acid	DNA	RNA	gene
clone	recombinant DNA	uracil	triplet
nitrogenous	genetic code	DNA fingerprint	autoradiograph
stem cell	PCR	deoxyribose	helix

1. The material that contains the information that determines inherited

characteristics is called _____.

2. The sugar in DNA is _____.

3. A(n) _____ is an organic compound, either RNA or DNA, whose molecules are made up of one or two chains of nucleotides that carry genetic information.

4. A(n) _____ is a segment of DNA in a chromosome that codes for a specific hereditary trait.

5. Protein synthesis begins with a cell making a(n) _____ strand that codes for a specific protein.

6. RNA has the base _____ instead of the base thymine found in DNA.

7. The _____ is a listing of the RNA triplets and their corresponding amino acids.

8. RNA is composed of four _____ bases.

9. The pattern of bands that results when a person's DNA sample is fragmented,

replicated, and separated is called a(n) _____.

10. A DNA strand is often found in the form of a double _____.

11. Scientists use a method called _____ to replicate a short sequence of double-stranded DNA.

12. A(n) _____ is an organism that is produced by asexual reproduction and that is genetically identical to its parent.

13. A(n) _____ is an undifferentiated cell that has not yet specialized to become a specific tissue in an animal.

5 Biological Chemistry

Concept Review *continued*

14. DNA molecules that are artificially created by combining DNA from different

sources is called _____.

15. Like a polysaccharide or a polypeptide, a(n) _____ is a biological
polymer.

16. A group of three RNA bases, called a(n) _____, indicates a partic-
ular amino acid.

17. An image that shows the DNA's pattern of nitrogenous bases is a(n)

_____.

18. Nucleic acids are formed from equal numbers of three chemical units: a sugar,

a phosphate group, and a(n) _____ base.

Answer the following items in the space provided.

19. How does DNA replicate itself?

_____

_____

_____

_____

_____

_____

20. A segment of DNA has the base sequence TAC TTT TCG AAG AGT ATT.

   a. What is the base sequence in a complementary strand of RNA?

   _____

   b. What is the corresponding amino acid sequence?

   _____

   c. What is the base sequence in a complementary strand of DNA?

   _____

Name _____ Class _____ Date _____

21. A segment of DNA has the base sequence TAC CTT ACA GAT TGT ACT.

    a. What is the base sequence in the complementary strand of RNA?

    _____

    b. What is the corresponding amino acid sequence?

    _____

    c. What is the base sequence in the complementary strand of DNA?

    _____

22. What is cloning, and how has it been accomplished in mammals?

    _____

    _____

    _____

    _____

Name _____ Class _____ Date _____

Concept Review

Section: Energy in Living Systems

Complete each statement below by choosing a term from the following list. Terms may be used more than once.

photosynthesis	respiration	ATP	chlorophyll
exothermic	glycolysis	Kreb's	synthetic
mechanical	transport	carbon	cellular

1. In the _____ cycle, reactions involving carbon compounds give plants and animals the energy they need.

2. Plants and animals use glucose to produce chemical energy in the form of a

   substance called _____ .

3. Green plants get energy directly from the sun's rays through a process called

   _____ .

4. Most plants use _____ , a magnesium-containing molecule, to capture the sun's energy.

5. The entire process of getting oxygen into body tissues and allowing it to react

   with glucose to generate energy is called _____ .

6. Chemical, or _____ , respiration takes place in the cells of a plant or animal and is fueled by glucose and oxygen.

7. Respiration is a(n) _____ process that gives off energy.

8. The first stage of cellular respiration involves _____ , in which a six-carbon glucose is split into two molecules.

9. The second stage of cellular respiration is called the _____ cycle, which forms carbon dioxide.

10. ATP gives the energy needed for _____ work, which allows muscles to flex and move .

11. ATP gives the energy needed for _____ work, which carries solutes across membranes.

12. ATP gives the energy needed for _____ work, which makes compounds that do not form spontaneously.

Answer the following items in the space provided.

13. How do plants use photosynthesis to gather energy?

_____

_____

_____

_____

_____

_____

14. Explain how animals indirectly gather energy from the sun.

_____

_____

_____

_____

_____

_____

15. How is cellular respiration the opposite of photosynthesis?

_____

_____

_____

_____

_____

_____

16. Describe the two stages of cellular respiration.

_____

_____

_____

_____

_____

_____

Assessment

Quiz

Section: Carbohydrates and Lipids

In the space provided, write the letter of the term or phrase that best answers the question.

_____ **1.** Most of your food energy comes from
   a. carbohydrates.
   b. proteins.
   c. lipids.
   d. cellulose.

_____ **2.** When your body digests starch, a product of the reaction is
   a. cellulose.
   b. maltose.
   c. glucose.
   d. a disaccharide.

_____ **3.** Which of the following are structural components of carbohydrates?
   a. hydroxyl groups
   b. rings containing carbon
   c. carbon, hydrogen, and oxygen
   d. All of the above

_____ **4.** The carbohydrates that living things use to store energy are
   a. monosaccharides and disaccharides.
   b. starch and glycogen.
   c. starch and chitin.
   d. starch and fats.

_____ **5.** The breakdown of polysaccharides to form monosaccharides is an example of what type of reaction?
   a. hydrolysis
   b. condensation
   c. substitution
   d. All of the above

_____ **6.** What is the general formula for a carbohydrate?
   a. $C_6H_{10}O_5$
   b. $C_{6n}H_{10}O_{5n+1}$
   c. $C_{6n}H_{10n+2}O_{5n+1}$
   d. $C_nH_{10n+2}O_{5n+1}$

Name _____ Class _____ Date _____

_____ **7.** Compounds used as sweeteners include
   a. glycogen and sugar.
   b. cellulose and sucrose.
   c. fructose and sucrose.
   d. polysaccharides.

_____ **8.** The human body uses glucose to
   a. store energy for a long time.
   b. break down cellulose molecules.
   c. build cellulose molecules.
   d. provide energy to cells.

_____ **9.** One byproduct of the formation of polysaccharides is
   a. oxygen.
   b. water.
   c. protein.
   d. Both (a) and (b)

_____ **10.** Cholesterol is an example of a
   a. monosaccharide.
   b. polysaccharide.
   c. lipid.
   d. biological polymer.

Assessment

Quiz

Section: Proteins

In the space provided, write the letter of the term or phrase that best answers the question.

_____ **1.** All protein molecules contain atoms of which elements?
  a. carbon, nitrogen, and oxygen
  b. carbon, sulfur, and oxygen
  c. carbon, nitrogen, and sulfur
  d. carbon, nitrogen, and iron

_____ **2.** Which of the following is a product of protein synthesis?
  a. ammonia
  b. nitrogen
  c. water
  d. oxygen

_____ **3.** The characteristic functional groups of a protein are
  a. $-OH$ and $-NH_2$.
  b. $-COOH$ and $-CH_2$.
  c. $-COOH$ and $-NH_2$.
  d. $-COOH$ and $-SH$.

_____ **4.** The symbol $-R$ in the structural formula of an amino acid represents
  a. a hydrogen atom.
  b. a side chain.
  c. an amino group.
  d. another amino acid.

_____ **5.** On a protein molecule, side chains of amino acids affect
  a. only the primary structure.
  b. only the secondary structure.
  c. primary, secondary, and tertiary structures.
  d. secondary, tertiary, and quaternary structures.

_____ **6.** What is the active site of an enzyme?
  a. the disulfide bridge
  b. the section of the molecule that interacts with a substrate
  c. the carboxylic acid group at the end of the protein chain
  d. a group of amino acids in the middle of the protein chain

Quiz *continued*

_____ **7.** The shape of a protein is determined by
   a. the sequence of amino acids.
   b. hydrogen bonding between sections of the molecule.
   c. disulfide bridges.
   d. All of the above

_____ **8.** The peptide bonds of a protein determine its
   a. primary structure.
   b. secondary structure.
   c. quaternary structure.
   d. All of the above

_____ **9.** The unique characteristic of the amino acid cysteine is
   a. a high level of acidity.
   b. its ability to form hydrogen bonds with other amino acids.
   c. its ability to form a chemical bond with another cysteine.
   d. a second amino group.

_____ **10.** An enzyme can be denatured by
   a. heating.
   b. interaction with a solvent.
   c. a very low pH.
   d. All of the above

Name _____ Class _____ Date _____

Quiz

Section: Nucleic Acids

In the space provided, write the letter of the term or phrase that best answers the question.

_____ 1. All the genetic information for an organism is stored in its
  a. proteins.
  b. nucleic acids.
  c. polypeptides.
  d. enzymes.

_____ 2. The components of a nucleic acid are
  a. sugars, phosphate groups, and amino acids.
  b. sugars, phosphate groups, and nitrogen-containing bases.
  c. sugars, amino acids, and nitrogen-containing bases.
  d. peptides, phosphate groups, and nitrogen-containing bases.

_____ 3. The symbol –TGCAGCAA– could represent a portion of
  a. a DNA molecule.
  b. an RNA molecule.
  c. Both (a) and (b)
  d. Neither (a) nor (b)

_____ 4. The two strands of a DNA molecule have
  a. bases in the same order.
  b. bases in a complementary order.
  c. an independent order of bases.
  d. a different number of bases.

_____ 5. The process by which DNA makes a copy of itself is called
  a. gene mapping.
  b. protein synthesis.
  c. DNA fingerprinting.
  d. replication.

_____ 6. The shape of a DNA molecule is described as
  a. a spring.
  b. a double helix.
  c. a crosslinked spiral.
  d. a double coil.

Name _____ Class _____ Date _____

Quiz *continued*

_____ **7.** How many amino acids are coded by this sequence
  –GGGCACAGAUGC?
  a. 1
  b. 3
  c. 4
  d. 12

_____ **8.** The polymerase chain reaction is used to
  a. make copies of a section of a DNA molecule.
  b. produce clones from stem cells.
  c. make an RNA "fingerprint."
  d. break a DNA molecule into small fragments.

_____ **9.** What determines the differences between a clone and its "parent"
  organism?
  a. minor differences in their DNA sequence
  b. nongenetic factors
  c. large differences in their RNA sequence
  d. All of the above

_____ **10.** What process is used to make bacteria that produce human insulin?
  a. cloning
  b. genetic fingerprinting
  c. recombinant DNA technology
  d. a series of polymerase chain reactions

Assessment

Quiz

Section: Energy in Living Systems

In the space provided, write the letter of the term or phrase that best answers the question.

_____ **1.** Plants use energy directly from sunlight during
  a. photosynthesis.
  b. respiration.
  c. the conversion of ATP to ADP.
  d. Both (a) and (b)

_____ **2.** The reactants in photosynthesis are
  a. oxygen and water.
  b. carbon dioxide and water.
  c. oxygen and carbon dioxide.
  d. oxygen, carbon dioxide, and water.

_____ **3.** The process of cellular respiration occurs
  a. in plant cells.
  b. in animal cells.
  c. only in chlorophyll producing plant cells.
  d. in both plant and animal cells.

_____ **4.** The reactants in cellular respiration are
  a. glucose and water.
  b. glucose and oxygen.
  c. glucose and carbon dioxide.
  d. carbon dioxide and water.

_____ **5.** Which part(s) of the carbon cycle are endothermic?
  a. photosynthesis
  b. cellular respiration
  c. Both (a) and (b)
  d. Neither (a) nor (b)

_____ **6.** The structural difference between ATP and ADP is
  a. the identity of the base.
  b. one water molecule.
  c. the charge on the ion.
  d. the number of phosphate groups.

_____ **7.** The hydrolysis of ATP is
  a. endothermic and spontaneous.
  b. endothermic and not spontaneous.
  c. exothermic and spontaneous.
  d. exothermic and not spontaneous.

_____ **8.** During the cellular respiration process, how many ATP ions are produced for each molecule of glucose?
  a. 1
  b. 6
  c. 20
  d. 38

_____ **9.** In plants, the products of cellular respiration are
  a. carbon dioxide and water.
  b. oxygen and water.
  c. carbon dioxide and glucose.
  d. oxygen and glucose.

_____ **10.** The enthalpy change of cellular respiration is
  a. positive.
  b. negative.
  c. zero.
  d. impossible to determine.

Assessment
Chapter Test

Biological Chemistry

In the space provided, write the letter of the term or phrase that best completes each statement or best answers each question.

_____ **1.** The monomer of both starch and cellulose is
  a. fructose.
  b. glucose.
  c. sucrose.
  d. maltose.

_____ **2.** The primary function of polysaccharides in animals is to
  a. store energy in chemical bonds.
  b. provide structural strength.
  c. carry oxygen to muscles.
  d. carry genetic information.

_____ **3.** When glycogen is broken down into sugar, what type of reaction occurs?
  a. condensation
  b. polymerization
  c. hydrolysis
  d. addition

_____ **4.** Waxes and fats are classified as
  a. polymers.
  b. lipids.
  c. carbohydrates.
  d. All of the above

_____ **5.** What two functional groups are necessary for a compound to be classified as an amino acid?
  a. $-CONH_2$ and $-CH_2$
  b. $-COOH$ and $-NH$
  c. $-COOH$ and $-NH_2$
  d. $-OH$ and $-CONH_2$

_____ **6.** One product of the reaction of amino acids to form a polypeptide is
  a. oxygen.
  b. ammonia.
  c. energy.
  d. water.

| Chapter Test *continued*

_____ **7.** Amino acid side chains can affect the shape of a protein by
    a. forming hydrogen bonds.
    b. forming chemical bonds.
    c. hydrophobic interactions.
    d. All of the above

_____ **8.** When an enzyme interacts with a substrate, the enzyme
    a. reacts with the substrate to form a new compound.
    b. undergoes a hydrolysis reaction.
    c. is not changed by the interaction.
    d. becomes denatured.

_____ **9.** When a protein is denatured by heat, it
    a. breaks apart into smaller peptide groups.
    b. loses its tertiary and quaternary structures.
    c. loses its primary structure.
    d. returns to its original form as it cools.

_____ **10.** Genetic information is stored in nucleic acids by the
    a. arrangement of the bases in a sequence.
    b. hydrogen bonding between bases.
    c. arrangement of sugars in a sequence.
    d. number of phosphate groups in the chain.

_____ **11.** A gene is a segment of DNA that holds the code for
    a. building a polypeptide.
    b. building an amino acid.
    c. building a carbohydrate.
    d. replicating itself.

_____ **12.** All of the following are examples of gene technology except
    a. DNA fingerprinting.
    b. cloning.
    c. using antibiotics to fight an infection.
    d. creating bacteria that manufacture drugs.

_____ **13.** In the endothermic chemical reaction, $6H_2O + 6CO_2 \rightarrow C_6H_{12}O_6 + 6O_2$, energy to drive the reaction comes from
    a. the conversion of ATP to ADP.
    b. heat.
    c. light.
    d. glycogen.

_____ **14.** The energy released by cellular respiration is carried by
    a. ADP.
    b. ATP.
    c. glucose.
    d. glycogen.

_____ **15.** Energy released by cellular respiration that is not stored chemically is released as
    a. a change in cell dimensions.
    b. heat.
    c. glucose.
    d. ATP.

_____ **16.** The sequence ACGUUGACCCA represents a segment of
    a. DNA.
    b. RNA.
    c. an enzyme.
    d. either DNA or RNA.

_____ **17.** How many RNA bases are necessary to code a protein that has 170 amino acid units?
    a. 170
    b. 340
    c. 510
    d. The number can vary depending on the specific amino acids.

_____ **18.** Sickle cell anemia is caused by a change in hemoglobin's
    a. primary structure.
    b. amino-acid sequence.
    c. secondary structure.
    d. All of the above

_____ **19.** The following biological molecules are all polymers, except
    a. cholesterol.
    b. glycogen.
    c. chitin.
    d. RNA.

_____ **20.** Energy carried by ATP is available to cells for
    a. chemical reactions.
    b. changing the shape of muscles.
    c. moving chemicals across the cell membrane.
    d. All of the above

| Chapter Test *continued*

Answer the following questions in the spaces provided.

21. Starch, glucose, glycogen and ATP each play a role in the energy transfer reactions in your body. Briefly explain the role of each compound.

_____

_____

_____

_____

22. Explain the role of DNA and RNA in the production of proteins.

_____

_____

_____

_____

23. Why is polymerase chain reaction an important part of the process of DNA fingerprinting?

_____

_____

_____

_____

24. How can two polypeptides have the same amino acids in the same order but have different properties?

_____

_____

_____

_____

Answer the following question on a separate piece of paper.

25. Write the general equations for photosynthesis and respiration. Explain why the sun can be considered the ultimate source of energy for animals, including carnivores, as well as plants.

Name _____ Class _____ Date _____

DATASHEET FOR IN-TEXT LAB

Denaturing an Enzyme

OBJECTIVE

Demonstrate the effect of heating on the nature of an enzyme.

MATERIALS

For each group of 2 to 3 students:

- beaker, 100 mL
- dropper
- hot plate
- hydrogen peroxide solution
- paper plate

- potato cubes
- stopwatch
- tongs
- water

Always wear safety goggles, gloves, and a lab apron to protect your eyes and clothing. If you get a chemical in your eyes, immediately flush the chemical out at the eyewash station while calling to your teacher. Know the location of the emergency lab shower and eyewash station and the procedures for using them.

Procedure

1. Get 15 potato cubes from your teacher. Place one potato cube on a paper plate.

2. Using a dropper, drop hydrogen peroxide solution onto the potato cube. Note the amount of bubbling (the enzymatic activity). Let this amount of bubbling count as a score of 10.

3. Place the remaining potato cubes in a beaker of water at room temperature. Place the beaker on a preheated hot plate that remains switched on.

4. Using tongs, remove one cube every 30 s and test its enzymatic activity, assigning a score between 0 and 10 based on the amount of bubbling.

Analysis

1. Graph the enzymatic activity score versus heating time.

   _____

   _____

2. What happens to the enzymatic activity of a potato with heating? Explain.

   _____

   _____

Name _____ Class _____ Date _____

Isolation of Onion DNA

OBJECTIVE

Extract DNA from the cells of an onion.

MATERIALS

For each group of 2 to 3 students:

- ethanol, ice-cold (5 mL)
- glass stirring rod
- onion extract (5 mL)
- pipet
- test tube
- test tube rack

Always wear safety goggles, gloves, and a lab apron to protect your eyes and clothing. If you get a chemical in your eyes, immediately flush the chemical out at the eyewash station while calling to your teacher. Know the location of the emergency lab shower and eyewash station and the procedures for using them.

Procedure

1. Place 5 mL of onion extract in a test tube. The extract was taken from whole onions that were processed in a laboratory.

2. Hold the test tube at a 45° angle. Use a pipet to add 5 mL of ice-cold ethanol to the tube, one drop at a time. Note: Allow the ethanol to run slowly down the side of the tube so that it forms a distinct layer.

3. Let the test tube stand for 2–3 min.

4. Insert a glass stirring rod into the boundary between the onion extract and the ethanol. Gently twirl the stirring rod by rolling the handle between your thumb and finger.

5. Remove the stirring rod from the liquids and examine any material that has stuck to it. You are looking at onion DNA. Touch the DNA to the lip of the test tube, and observe how it acts as you try to remove it.

Analysis

1. Why do you think the DNA is now visible?

_____

_____

2. How has the DNA changed from when it was undisturbed in the onion's cells?

_____

_____

Name _____ Class _____ Date _____

All Fats Are Not Equal

In a saturated fatty acid, each carbon atom is connected to its neighbors by single bonds, while in an unsaturated fatty acid, some carbon atoms are connected by double bonds. The number of carbon-carbon double bonds in a molecule is the substance's degree of unsaturation. The degree of unsaturation and the total number of carbon atoms in the fatty acid chains determine the differences between fats and oils. For example, myristic acid is a solid at room temperature according to the **Information Table,** but oleic acid, which has one carbon-carbon double bond, is a liquid. Similarly, you should notice an increase in melting points as you move from myristic acid to stearic acid because the number of carbon atoms increases. In general, at room temperature, fats are solids and oils are liquids. Therefore, you might predict a fat to be mostly saturated fatty acids and an oil to be mainly unsaturated fatty acids.

To determine the degree of unsaturation, scientists test for the amount of iodine that reacts with a 100 g sample of fat or oil. This value is the iodine number. The higher the value of the iodine number, the greater the amount of unsaturation in the fat or oil. When I_2 is added to the colorless fat or oil, the mixture appears red violet, like I_2. During the reaction, the color of the mixture fades as I_2 adds to the carbon-carbon double bond, producing a colorless product.

INFORMATION TABLE—REPRESENTATIVE FATTY ACIDS OF DIETARY FATS AND OILS

Fatty acid	Melting point (°C)	Class (saturated or unsaturated)	Molecular structure
Myristic acid	58	Saturated	$CH_3—(CH_2)_{12}—CO_2H$
Palmitic acid	63	Saturated	$CH_3—(CH_2)_{14}—CO_2H$
Stearic acid	71	Saturated	$CH_3—(CH_2)_{16}—CO_2H$
Oleic acid	16	Monounsaturated	$CH_3—(CH_2)_7—CH=CH—(CH_2)_7—CO_2H$
Linoleic acid	−5	Polyunsaturated	$CH_3—(CH_2)_4—CH=CH—CH_2—CH=CH—(CH_2)_7—CO_2H$
Linolenic acid	−11	Polyunsaturated	$CH_3—CH_2—CH=CH—CH_2—CH=CH—CH_2—CH=CH—(CH_2)_7—CO_2H$

OBJECTIVES

Determine the degree of unsaturation in fatty acids.

Relate how melting point indicates the degree of saturation.

All Fats Are Not Equal *continued*

MATERIALS

- beaker, 500 mL
- beaker tongs
- beakers, 25 mL (6)
- butter
- coconut oil
- cod liver oil
- corn oil
- gloves
- graduated cylinders, 25 mL (5)
- hot plate
- lab apron
- milk chocolate, 1 in. × 0.25 in. piece
- peanut oil
- ring stand
- safety goggles
- soft margarine
- spatula
- stick margarine
- sunflower oil
- tablespoon
- test-tube rack
- test tubes, medium (10)
- thermometer
- thermometer clamp
- tincture of iodine
- vegetable shortening
- wax pencil

  Always wear safety goggles, gloves, and a lab apron to protect your eyes and clothing. If you get a chemical in your eyes, immediately flush the chemical out at the eyewash station while calling to your teacher. Know the location of the emergency lab shower and eyewash station and the procedures for using them.

Do not touch any chemicals. If you get a chemical on your skin or clothing, wash the chemical off at the sink while calling to your teacher. Make sure you carefully read the labels and follow the precautions on all containers of chemicals that you use. If there are no precautions stated on the label, ask your teacher what precautions to follow. Do not taste any chemicals or items used in the laboratory. Never return leftover chemicals to their original containers; take only small amounts to avoid wasting supplies.

Call your teacher in the event of a spill. Spills should be cleaned up promptly, according to your teacher's directions.

Never put broken glass in a regular waste container. Broken glass should be disposed of separately according to your teacher's instructions. **Never stir with a thermometer because the glass around the bulb is fragile and might break.**

| All Fats Are Not Equal *continued*

Procedure

PART 1–DETERMINING THE DEGREE OF UNSATURATION IN COMMERCIALLY AVAILABLE OILS

1. Put on safety goggles, gloves, and a lab apron.

2. Use a wax pencil to label five individual test tubes "Peanut oil," "Sunflower oil," "Corn oil," "Cod liver oil," and "Coconut oil."

3. Using a graduated cylinder, measure 10 mL of peanut oil and pour it into the appropriately labeled test tube. Set the test tube in a test-tube rack. Do the same for each of the other four oils.

4. Add two drops of tincture of iodine to each labeled test tube. *Carefully* swirl each test tube to disperse the iodine into small droplets. Return the test tube to the test-tube rack.

5. Let each mixture of oil and iodine stand for at least 10 minutes. Note the time it takes for any color change to occur *after* adding the iodine. Record both the time and color change in **Table 1.**

6. Determine an "unsaturation ranking" for this set of oil samples based on whether a color change occurs (red violet to colorless). If a color change occurs, record the elapsed time. Record your ranking in **Table 1.**

PART 2–DETERMINING THE MELTING POINT OF FOODSTUFFS AND THE DEGREE OF FATTY ACID SATURATION

7. Use a wax pencil to label six individual beakers "Vegetable shortening," "Butter," "Corn oil," "Margarine," "Soft margarine," and "Chocolate."

8. Measure a *level* tablespoon (5 g) of each soft food sample, and place it in its correspondingly labeled beaker. Use a spatula to help level each soft food sample. Place the piece of chocolate in its beaker.

9. Using **Figure 1** as a guide, prepare a water bath. Place one of the beakers prepared in **step 8** in the water bath. Heat on the hot plate's low setting, so that the temperature of the water gradually increases from room temperature. Monitor the temperature. Record the temperature at which the food sample liquefies completely in **Table 2.** Using beaker tongs, remove the warmed sample from the water bath. Repeat for each food sample. Record the room temperature for corn oil.

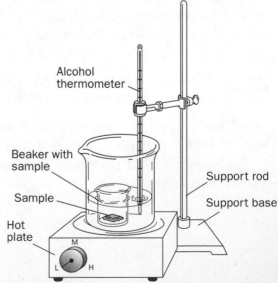

Alcohol thermometer

Beaker with sample

Sample

Hot plate

Support rod

Support base

Figure 1

Name _____ Class _____ Date _____

| All Fats Are Not Equal *continued*

10. For each sample tested, review the fatty acid ingredients listed in **Table 2** and your melting-point data. Then rank each food sample from highest saturated fatty acid content to lowest saturated fatty acid content. Record this ranking in **Table 2.**

11. Clean all apparatus and your lab station. Return equipment to its proper place. Dispose of your materials according to your teacher's directions. Dispose of chemicals and waste oils in containers designated by your teacher. Do not pour any chemicals or oils down the drain or put them in the trash unless your teacher directs you to do so. Wash your hands thoroughly after all work is finished and before you leave the lab.

TABLE 1 DETERMINING THE DEGREE OF UNSATURATION IN OILS

Oil type	Number of iodine (I_2) drops	Time to change color (min)	Color change ($\checkmark$)	Analysis ranking (most unsaturated to least) 1–5
Peanut oil				
Sunflower oil				
Corn oil				
Cod liver oil				
Coconut oil				

TABLE 2 MELTING POINT AND DEGREE OF SATURATION

Food sample	Melting point (°C)	Fatty acid ingredient(s)	Analysis ranking (most unsaturated to least)
Vegetable shortening		Hydrogenated and partially hydrogenated vegetable oils	
Butter		Palmitic acid (29%), oleic acid (27%)	
Stick margarine		Partially hydrogenated vegetable oils	
Soft margarine		Partially hydrogenated vegetable oils	
Corn oil		Polyunsaturated acids (34%), oleic acid (50%)	
Chocolate		Palmitic acid (24%), stearic acid (35%), oleic acid (38%)	

All Fats Are Not Equal *continued*

Analysis

1. **Analyzing Data** Examine your entries in **Table 1.** What trend do you observe in vegetable oils regarding unsaturated fatty acid side chains?

_____

_____

2. **Analyzing Data and Applying Concepts** Coconut oil is a major ingredient in many nondairy creamers and other prepared foods. If an individual is trying to reduce saturated fat intake, would a nondairy creamer containing coconut oil be a good choice? Explain.

_____

_____

_____

Lesson Plan

Section: Carbohydrates and Lipids

Pacing

Regular Schedule	**with lab(s):** 2 days	**without lab(s):** 1 day
Block Schedule	**with lab(s):** 1 day	**without lab(s):** ½ day

Objectives

1. Describe the structure of carbohydrates.

2. Relate the structure of carbohydrates to their role in biological systems.

3. Identify the reactions that lead to the formation and breakdown of carbohydrate polymers.

4. Describe a property that all lipids share.

National Science Education Standards Covered

UNIFYING CONCEPTS AND PROCESSES

UCP 1 Systems, order, and organization

UCP 2 Evidence, models, and explanation

UCP 3 Change, constancy, and measurement

PHYSICAL SCIENCE—STRUCTURE AND PROPERTIES OF MATTER

PS 2f Carbon atoms can bond to one another in chains, rings, and branching networks to form a variety of structures, including synthetic polymers, oils, and the large molecules essential to life.

PHYSICAL SCIENCE—CHEMICAL REACTIONS

PS 3a Chemical reactions occur all around us, for example in health care, cooking, cosmetics, and automobiles. Complex chemical reactions involving carbon-based molecules take place constantly in every cell in our bodies.

> **KEY**
> **SE** = Student Edition
> **ATE** = Annotated Teacher Edition

Block 1 *(45 minutes)*

FOCUS *5 minutes*

❑ **Bellringer,** ATE (GENERAL). This activity has students write the complete combustion reaction for cellulose.

MOTIVATE *10 minutes*

❑ **Demonstration,** ATE (GENERAL). This demonstration illustrates how to test for simple sugars using Benedict's solution.

Lesson Plan *continued*

TEACH *20 minutes*

❑ **Real-World Connection,** ATE (BASIC). Show students the label of a product that contains aspartame; use the questions in this feature to discuss the properties of aspartame.

❑ **Skill Builder,** ATE (GENERAL). Have students write the balanced chemical equation for the hydrolysis of sucrose, and calculate the mass of fructose formed from the hydrolysis of 2.5 moles of sucrose.

❑ **Teaching Tip,** ATE (BASIC). Use models to show students the chemistry behind the condensation reaction that forms sucrose.

❑ **Consumer Lab: All Fats Are Not Created Equal,** (GENERAL). Students evaluate samples of different fatty acids to determine the degree of unsaturation of each. They then relate how the melting point of each fatty acid indicates the degree of saturation.

CLOSE *10 minutes*

❑ **Reteaching,** ATE (BASIC). Use a ball-and-stick model of two glucose molecules and have students identify the groups on each molecule.

❑ **Quiz,** ATE (GENERAL). This assignment has students answer questions about the concepts in this lesson.

❑ **Assessment Worksheet: Section Quiz** (GENERAL)

HOMEWORK

❑ **Reading Skill Builder,** ATE (BASIC). Have students list things that they already know about biological reactions.

❑ **Homework,** ATE (GENERAL). This assignment has students examine nutrition labels and determine the number of carbohydrates in one serving.

❑ **Section Review,** SE (GENERAL). Assign items 1–13.

❑ **Skills Worksheet: Concept Review** (GENERAL)

OTHER RESOURCES

❑ **Skill Builder,** ATE (ADVANCED). Use this exercise to reinforce the everyday relevance of molar-based calculations.

❑ **go.hrw.com**

❑ **www.scilinks.org**

Lesson Plan

Section: Proteins

Pacing

Regular Schedule	**with lab(s):** NA	**without lab(s):** 2 days
Block Schedule	**with lab(s):** NA	**without lab(s):** 1 day

Objectives

1. Describe amino acid structure.

2. Explain how amino acids form proteins through condensation.

3. Explain the significance of amino-acid side chains to the three-dimensional structure and function of a protein.

4. Describe how enzymes work and how the structure and function of an enzyme is affected by changes in temperature and pH.

National Science Education Standards Covered

UNIFYING CONCEPTS AND PROCESSES

UCP 1 Systems, order, and organization

UCP 2 Evidence, models, and explanation

UCP 5 Form and function

PHYSICAL SCIENCE—STRUCTURE AND PROPERTIES OF MATTER

PS 2f Carbon atoms can bond to one another in chains, rings, and branching networks to form a variety of structures, including synthetic polymers, oils, and the large molecules essential to life.

PHYSICAL SCIENCE—CHEMICAL REACTIONS

PS 3a Chemical reactions occur all around us, for example in health care, cooking, cosmetics, and automobiles. Complex chemical reactions involving carbon-based molecules take place constantly in every cell in our bodies.

PS 3e Catalysts, such as metal surfaces, accelerate chemical reactions. Chemical reactions in living systems are catalyzed by protein molecules called enzymes.

KEY
SE = Student Edition
ATE = Annotated Teacher Edition

Block 2 *(45 minutes)*

FOCUS *10 minutes*

❏ **Bellringer** ATE (GENERAL). This activity has students determine how many ways 20-piece sets of 20 different objects can be arranged into a 20-object long sequence.

| Lesson Plan *continued*

MOTIVATE *10 minutes*

❑ **Demonstration,** ATE (GENERAL). This demonstration uses ball-and-stick models to visualize amino acids and to understand their structure and properties.

TEACH *25 minutes*

❑ **Using the Table,** ATE (GENERAL). This activity has students compare the structures of amino acids in Table 2 and derive a general structure for an amino acid.

❑ **Using the Figure,** ATE (GENERAL). Use the questions in this feature to help students examine the interactions shown in Figure 6.

❑ **Teaching Tip,** ATE (GENERAL). This activity has students learn the roots *hydro-* and *-phobic*.

❑ **Discussion,** ATE (GENERAL). This feature has students compare examples of shape-dependent processes with amino acid structures and shapes.

HOMEWORK

❑ **Reading Skill Builder,** ATE (BASIC). This activity has students draw a concept map for the terms and concepts in this section.

❑ **Homework,** ATE (BASIC). This assignment has students create a graphic organizer using the following terms: protein structure, protein function, denaturation, primary structure, tertiary structure, amino acid substitution, and quaternary structure.

OTHER RESOURCES

❑ **Skill Builder,** ATE (ADVANCED). Have the students make a written narrative of the process they use to determine the four levels of structure of an unknown protein.

❑ **Focus on Graphing,** SE (GENERAL).

❑ **go.hrw.com**

❑ **www.scilinks.org**

Block 3 *(45 minutes)*

TEACH *30 minutes*

❑ **Transparency,** Levels of Protein Structure (GENERAL). This transparency illustrates the four levels of protein structure. (Table 3)

❑ **Demonstration,** ATE (BASIC). This demonstration illustrates how heat can denature a protein found in pineapple juice.

❑ **Transparency,** Enzyme Mechanism (GENERAL). This transparency illustrates how an enzyme reacts with a substrate. (Figure 8)

❑ **Quick Lab: Denaturing an Enzyme,** SE (GENERAL). This lab has students test the effect of heat on enzymes in potato based on the amount of bubbling produced when hydrogen peroxide is applied. Students then answer two analysis questions about what they have done.

Lesson Plan *continued*

CLOSE *15 minutes*

❑ **Quiz,** ATE (GENERAL). This assignment has students answer questions about the concepts in this lesson.

❑ **Reteaching,** ATE (BASIC). Use this demonstration to discuss the intermolecular forces that give proteins their unique shapes.

❑ **Assessment Worksheet: Section Quiz** (GENERAL)

HOMEWORK

❑ **Skills Worksheet: Concept Review** (GENERAL). Review the main concepts and problem-solving skills of this section by having students do this worksheet in class.

❑ **Section Review,** SE (GENERAL). Assign items 1–12.

OTHER RESOURCES

❑ **Skills Builder,** ATE (ADVANCED). This activity has students calculate the time required for 1000 carbonic anhydrase molecules to hydrate to 1.0 mol of carbonic acid.

❑ **go.hrw.com**

❑ **www.scilinks.org**

Lesson Plan

Section: Nucleic Acids

Pacing

Regular Schedule	**with lab(s):** NA	**without lab(s):** 2 days
Block Schedule	**with lab(s):** NA	**without lab(s):** 1 day

Objectives

1. Relate the structure of nucleic acids to their function as carriers of genetic information.

2. Describe how DNA uses the genetic code to control the synthesis of proteins.

3. Describe important gene technologies and their significance in modern technology.

National Science Education Standards Covered
UNIFYING CONCEPTS AND PROCESSES

UCP 1 Systems, order, and organization

UCP 2 Evidence, models, and explanation

UCP 5 Form and function

PHYSICAL SCIENCE—STRUCTURE AND PROPERTIES OF MATTER

PS 2f Carbon atoms can bond to one another in chains, rings, and branching networks to form a variety of structures, including synthetic polymers, oils, and the large molecules essential to life.

KEY
SE = Student Edition
ATE = Annotated Teacher Edition

Block 4 *(45 minutes)*
FOCUS *10 minutes*

❑ **Bellringer** ATE (GENERAL). This activity has students consider the similarities between their parents and themselves.

MOTIVATE *5 minutes*

❑ **Using the Figure,** ATE (BASIC). Have students examine Figure 9 and compare the structures.

TEACH *30 minutes*

❑ **Using the Figure,** ATE (GENERAL). Point out the hydrogen bonding between base pairs in the DNA molecule shown in Figure 10.

❑ **Transparency,** Structure of DNA. (GENERAL) This transparency illustrates that the three-dimensional structure of DNA is held stable by hydrogen bonding between base pairs. (Figure 10)

❑ **Group Activity,** ATE (BASIC). This activity has students play a game using index cards and the four nitrogenous bases found in DNA.

❑ **Quick Lab: Isolation of Onion DNA,** SE (GENERAL). This lab has students isolate DNA from onion extract. Students then answer two analysis questions about what they have done.

HOMEWORK

❑ **Section Review,** SE (GENERAL). Assign items 1, 2, and 7–9.

OTHER RESOURCES

❑ **Discussion,** ATE (ADVANCED). This activity has students engage in a discussion regarding the use of DNA analysis of individuals with a disease. Students then research topics such as the Human Genome Project.

❑ **go.hrw.com**

❑ **www.scilinks.org**

Block 5 *(45 minutes)*

TEACH *30 minutes*

❑ **Transparency,** DNA Replication (GENERAL). This transparency illustrates how DNA replicates by building complementary strands on the single strands that form as the original helix unwinds. (Figure 12)

❑ **Teaching Tip,** ATE (GENERAL). Discuss with students how the unzipping of a zipper is an imperfect analogy for DNA replication.

❑ **Teaching Tip,** ATE (GENERAL). Use figures taken from a biology textbook to discuss protein synthesis.

❑ **Skills Toolkit: Using the Genetic Code,** SE (GENERAL). Use this feature to walk students through decoding a strand of RNA into amino acids.

❑ **Transparency,** Using the Genetic Code (GENERAL). This transparency illustrates how to use the table showing the genetic code. (Skills Toolkit 1)

Lesson Plan *continued*

CLOSE *15 minutes*

❑ **Reteaching,** ATE (BASIC). Students use Skills Toolkit 1 to determine the amino acid sequence and complementary DNA sequence of strings of DNA.

❑ **Quiz,** ATE (GENERAL). This assignment has students answer questions about the concepts in this lesson.

❑ **Assessment Worksheet: Section Quiz** (GENERAL)

HOMEWORK

❑ **Skills Worksheet: Concept Review** (GENERAL) Review the main concepts and problem-solving skills of this section by having students do this worksheet in class.

❑ **Homework,** ATE (GENERAL). This assignment provides additional practice using the genetic code.

❑ **Section Review,** SE (GENERAL). Assign items 3, 4–6, and 10.

OTHER RESOURCES

❑ **Demonstration,** ATE (GENERAL). This demonstration uses string and tooth-picks to model the double helix shape of DNA.

❑ **Using the Figure,** ATE (GENERAL). Use Figure 15 to discuss why the calico cat in the figure is not identical to its parent although it is genetically identical.

❑ **go.hrw.com**

❑ **www.scilinks.org**

Lesson Plan

Section: Energy in Living Systems

Pacing

Regular Schedule	with lab(s): NA	without lab(s): 2 days
Block Schedule	with lab(s): NA	without lab(s): 1 day

Objectives

1. Explain how plants use photosynthesis to gather energy.

2. Explain how plants and animals use energy from respiration to carry out biological functions.

National Science Education Standards Covered

UNIFYING CONCEPTS AND PROCESSES

UCP 1 Systems, order, and organization

UCP 2 Evidence, models, and explanation

UCP 3 Change, constancy, and measurement

PHYSICAL SCIENCE—CHEMICAL REACTIONS

PS 3a Chemical reactions occur all around us, for example in health care, cooking, cosmetics, and automobiles. Complex chemical reactions involving carbon-based molecules take place constantly in every cell in our bodies.

KEY
SE = Student Edition
ATE = Annotated Teacher Edition

Block 6 *(45 minutes)*

FOCUS *10 minutes*

❏ **Bellringer** ATE (GENERAL). Students answer questions about energy and living systems.

MOTIVATE *10 minutes*

❏ **Activity,** ATE (GENERAL). Small groups of students construct a large drawing of the carbon cycle and consider factors that affect it.

Lesson Plan *continued*

TEACH *25 minutes*

❏ **Skill Builder,** ATE (GENERAL). Students calculate the number of moles of glucose formed from photosynthesis of 132 g of carbon dioxide.

❏ **Transparency,** Photosynthesis and Respiration (GENERAL). This transparency illustrates how photosynthesis and cellular respiration are part of the carbon cycle. (Figure 15)

❏ **Reading Skill Builder,** ATE (BASIC). Students read the last two pages of this section in pairs and then summarize the concepts in their own words.

HOMEWORK

❏ **Homework,** ATE. This assignment has students produce a graphic organizer or concept map to show the relationship between the following words: energy storage, conversion of ATP to ADP, energy production, cellular respiration, glucose, and glycogen.

❏ **Section Review,** SE (GENERAL). Assign items 1–3, 6, and 7.

OTHER RESOURCES

❏ **Activity,** ATE (ADVANCED). Divide the class into groups. Have each group construct a large-sized drawing of the carbon cycle.

❏ **Teaching Tip,** ATE (ADVANCED). Students calculate the energy released when a 35 g glucose sugar cube is oxidized through cellular respiration.

❏ **go.hrw.com**

❏ **www.scilinks.org**

Block 7 *(45 minutes)*

TEACH *25 minutes*

❏ **Activity,** ATE (BASIC). This activity has students color code the complete reaction equations for photosynthesis and cellular respiration.

❏ **Group Activity,** ATE (GENERAL). This activity has students use models to visualize the reaction that takes place during cellular respiration.

❏ **Skill Builder,** ATE. Students use the data in Table 4 to create a bar graph showing the amount of energy required in kJ to do several different activities.

CLOSE *20 minutes*

❏ **Reteaching,** ATE (BASIC). Students draw a diagram of the carbon cycle and label the flow of energy through the system.

❏ **Quiz,** ATE (GENERAL). This assignment has students answer questions about the concepts in this lesson.

❏ **Assessment Worksheet: Section Quiz** (GENERAL)

Lesson Plan *continued*

HOMEWORK

❑ **Skills Worksheet: Concept Review** (GENERAL) Review the main concepts and problem-solving skills of this section by having students do this worksheet in class.

❑ **Section Review,** SE (GENERAL). Assign items 4, 5, and 8–10.

OTHER RESOURCES

❑ **go.hrw.com**

❑ **www.scilinks.org**

END OF CHAPTER REVIEW AND ASSESSMENT RESOURCES

❑ **Mixed Review,** SE (GENERAL).

❑ **Alternate Assessment,** SE (GENERAL).

❑ **Technology and Learning,** SE (GENERAL).

❑ **Standardized Test Prep,** SE (GENERAL).

❑ **Assessment Worksheet: Chapter Test** (GENERAL)

❑ **Test Item Listing for ExamView® Test Generator**

Name _____ Class _____ Date _____

Quick Lab

DATASHEET FOR IN-TEXT LAB

Denaturing an Enzyme

OBJECTIVE

Demonstrate the effect of heating on the nature of an enzyme.

MATERIALS

For each group of 2 to 3 students:

- beaker, 100 mL
- dropper
- hot plate
- hydrogen peroxide solution
- paper plate
- potato cubes
- stopwatch
- tongs
- water

Always wear safety goggles, gloves, and a lab apron to protect your eyes and clothing. If you get a chemical in your eyes, immediately flush the chemical out at the eyewash station while calling to your teacher. Know the location of the emergency lab shower and eyewash station and the procedures for using them.

Procedure

1. Get 15 potato cubes from your teacher. Place one potato cube on a paper plate.

2. Using a dropper, drop hydrogen peroxide solution onto the potato cube. Note the amount of bubbling (the enzymatic activity). Let this amount of bubbling count as a score of 10.

3. Place the remaining potato cubes in a beaker of water at room temperature. Place the beaker on a preheated hot plate that remains switched on.

4. Using tongs, remove one cube every 30 s and test its enzymatic activity, assigning a score between 0 and 10 based on the amount of bubbling.

Analysis

1. Graph the enzymatic activity score versus heating time.

   Answers may vary. Graphs should show a decrease in enzymatic activity as

   heating time increases.

2. What happens to the enzymatic activity of a potato with heating? Explain.

   Enzymatic activity decreases with heating time. Heat denatures the enzyme

   so that it no longer breaks down the hydrogen peroxide.

Name _____ Class _____ Date _____

Quick Lab

Isolation of Onion DNA

OBJECTIVE

Extract DNA from the cells of an onion.

MATERIALS

For each group of 2 to 3 students:

- ethanol, ice-cold (5 mL)
- glass stirring rod
- onion extract (5 mL)
- pipet
- test tube
- test tube rack

Always wear safety goggles, gloves, and a lab apron to protect your eyes and clothing. If you get a chemical in your eyes, immediately flush the chemical out at the eyewash station while calling to your teacher. Know the location of the emergency lab shower and eyewash station and the procedures for using them.

Procedure

1. Place 5 mL of onion extract in a test tube. The extract was taken from whole onions that were processed in a laboratory.

2. Hold the test tube at a 45° angle. Use a pipet to add 5 mL of ice-cold ethanol to the tube, one drop at a time. Note: Allow the ethanol to run slowly down the side of the tube so that it forms a distinct layer.

3. Let the test tube stand for 2–3 min.

4. Insert a glass stirring rod into the boundary between the onion extract and the ethanol. Gently twirl the stirring rod by rolling the handle between your thumb and finger.

5. Remove the stirring rod from the liquids and examine any material that has stuck to it. You are looking at onion DNA. Touch the DNA to the lip of the test tube, and observe how it acts as you try to remove it.

Analysis

1. Why do you think the DNA is now visible?

   The DNA is concentrated. That is, there are now many denatured DNA

   molecules clumped together so that you can see them.

2. How has the DNA changed from when it was undisturbed in the onion's cells?

   It is denatured and concentrated in long visible strings. It is not visible to

   the unaided eye when undisturbed in the cells.

Skills Practice Lab

CONSUMER

All Fats Are Not Equal

Teacher Notes

TIME REQUIRED One 45-minute lab period

SKILLS ACQUIRED
Collecting data
Communicating
Experimenting
Identifying patterns
Inferring
Interpreting
Organizing and analyzing data

RATING
Easy ◀——— 1   2   3   4 ——▶ Hard

Teacher Prep–3
Student Set-Up–3
Concept Level–2
Clean Up–3

THE SCIENTIFIC METHOD

Make Observations Using common household fats, students will determine the degree of saturation in fatty acids and relate the degree of saturation to melting point.

Analyze the Results Analysis questions 1 to 4

Draw Conclusions Analysis questions 1 and 2

Communicate the Results Analysis questions 1 and 2

MATERIALS

Wear safety goggles, disposable polyethylene gloves, and an apron when you prepare the iodine tincture solution. Work in a chemical fume hood known to be in operating condition and have another person stand by to call for help in case of an emergency. Be sure you are within a 30 second walk from a working safety shower and eyewash station.

To prepare 100 mL of tincture of iodine, add 7 g of I_2 crystals and 5 g of KI to 5 mL of distilled water, and dilute to 100 mL with denatured ethyl alcohol.

SAFETY CAUTIONS

Read all safety precautions, and discuss them with your students.

Safety goggles, gloves, and an apron must be worn at all times.

Broken glass should be disposed of in a clearly labeled box lined with a plastic trash bag. When the box is full, close it, seal it with packaging tape, and set it next to the trash can for disposal.

CAUTION: Tincture of iodine is a flammable liquid and a powerful stain. Avoid open flames or sparks. Have students handle with care.

All Fats Are Not Equal *continued*

Remind students of the following safety precautions:

- Always wear safety goggles, gloves, and a lab apron to protect your eyes and clothing. If you get a chemical in your eyes, immediately flush the chemical out at the eyewash station while calling to your teacher. Know the location of the emergency lab shower and the eyewash stations and procedures for using them.

- Do not touch any chemicals. If you get a chemical on your skin or clothing, wash the chemical off at the sink while calling to your teacher. Make sure you carefully read the labels and follow the precautions on all containers of chemicals that you use. If there are no precautions stated on the label, ask your teacher what precautions you should follow. Do not taste any chemicals or items used in the laboratory. Never return leftover chemicals to their original containers; take only small amounts to avoid wasting supplies.

- Call your teacher in the event of a spill. Spills should be cleaned up promptly, according to your teacher's directions.

- Never put broken glass in a regular waste container. Broken glass should be disposed of properly.

DISPOSAL

Dispose of solid foodstuffs as an inert solid waste. Collect liquid oil mixtures and mix thoroughly with 25 to 50 mL of liquid detergent to disperse the oils, and pour down the drain with copious amounts of water.

TIPS AND TRICKS

A single graduated cylinder can be used if it is washed and rinsed between samples to avoid mixing of oils.

If a change does not occur in the sunflower or cod liver oil (these oils have the highest iodine number and will shift color first) within 10 minutes at room temperature, have students place all the samples in a water bath and apply low heat. Within a few minutes, both these oils should turn colorless.

It is important to add initially the same amount of iodine to each of the oils. If the addition of iodine does not turn all oils immediately red-violet, continue adding iodine drop by drop.

Depending on the brand used, some students may rank sunflower oil as having the lowest ranking in **Table 1.**

In Part 2, it is important to start heating at a temperature below 32°C so that an accurate melting point can be determined for all solids.

Discuss the iodine number and how it indicates unsaturation. The iodine number is the number of grams of iodine that react with 100 grams of fat. Iodine numbers for the oils in Part 1 are: cod liver oil 135–165, sunflower oil 125–135, corn oil 110–130, peanut oil 90–100, coconut oil 6–10.

Student's data are qualitative, not quantitative. Although students do not calculate an actual iodine number, the color shift observed and the number of drops of iodine solution used allow an assessment of a generalized ranking. Results may vary according to product brands.

Students may benefit from a discussion of the table in the introduction.

Review the water-bath setup.

Name _____ Class _____ Date _____

Skills Practice Lab)   **CONSUMER**

All Fats Are Not Equal

In a saturated fatty acid, each carbon atom is connected to its neighbors by single bonds, while in an unsaturated fatty acid, some carbon atoms are connected by double bonds. The number of carbon-carbon double bonds in a molecule is the substance's degree of unsaturation. The degree of unsaturation and the total number of carbon atoms in the fatty acid chains determine the differences between fats and oils. For example, myristic acid is a solid at room temperature according to the **Information Table,** but oleic acid, which has one carbon-carbon double bond, is a liquid. Similarly, you should notice an increase in melting points as you move from myristic acid to stearic acid because the number of carbon atoms increases. In general, at room temperature, fats are solids and oils are liquids. Therefore, you might predict a fat to be mostly saturated fatty acids and an oil to be mainly unsaturated fatty acids.

To determine the degree of unsaturation, scientists test for the amount of iodine that reacts with a 100 g sample of fat or oil. This value is the iodine number. The higher the value of the iodine number, the greater the amount of unsaturation in the fat or oil. When I_2 is added to the colorless fat or oil, the mixture appears red violet, like I_2. During the reaction, the color of the mixture fades as I_2 adds to the carbon-carbon double bond, producing a colorless product.

INFORMATION TABLE—REPRESENTATIVE FATTY ACIDS OF DIETARY FATS AND OILS

Fatty acid	Melting point (°C)	Class (saturated or unsaturated)	Molecular structure
Myristic acid	58	Saturated	$CH_3-(CH_2)_{12}-CO_2H$
Palmitic acid	63	Saturated	$CH_3-(CH_2)_{14}-CO_2H$
Stearic acid	71	Saturated	$CH_3-(CH_2)_{16}-CO_2H$
Oleic acid	16	Monounsaturated	$CH_3-(CH_2)_7-CH=CH-(CH_2)_7-CO_2H$
Linoleic acid	−5	Polyunsaturated	$CH_3-(CH_2)_4-CH=CH-CH_2-CH=CH-(CH_2)_7-CO_2H$
Linolenic acid	−11	Polyunsaturated	$CH_3-CH_2-CH=CH-CH_2-CH=CH-CH_2-CH=CH-(CH_2)_7-CO_2H$

OBJECTIVES

Determine the degree of unsaturation in fatty acids.

Relate how melting point indicates the degree of saturation.

Name _____ Class _____ Date _____

All Fats Are Not Equal *continued*

MATERIALS

- beaker, 500 mL
- beaker tongs
- beakers, 25 mL (6)
- butter
- coconut oil
- cod liver oil
- corn oil
- gloves
- graduated cylinders, 25 mL (5)
- hot plate
- lab apron
- milk chocolate, 1 in. × 0.25 in. piece
- peanut oil
- ring stand

- safety goggles
- soft margarine
- spatula
- stick margarine
- sunflower oil
- tablespoon
- test-tube rack
- test tubes, medium (10)
- thermometer
- thermometer clamp
- tincture of iodine
- vegetable shortening
- wax pencil

 Always wear safety goggles, gloves, and a lab apron to protect your eyes and clothing. If you get a chemical in your eyes, immediately flush the chemical out at the eyewash station while calling to your teacher. Know the location of the emergency lab shower and eyewash station and the procedures for using them.

 Do not touch any chemicals. If you get a chemical on your skin or clothing, wash the chemical off at the sink while calling to your teacher. Make sure you carefully read the labels and follow the precautions on all containers of chemicals that you use. If there are no precautions stated on the label, ask your teacher what precautions to follow. Do not taste any chemicals or items used in the laboratory. Never return leftover chemicals to their original containers; take only small amounts to avoid wasting supplies.

Call your teacher in the event of a spill. Spills should be cleaned up promptly, according to your teacher's directions.

Never put broken glass in a regular waste container. Broken glass should be disposed of separately according to your teacher's instructions. **Never stir with a thermometer because the glass around the bulb is fragile and might break.**

Name _____ Class _____ Date _____

All Fats Are Not Equal *continued*

Procedure

PART 1–DETERMINING THE DEGREE OF UNSATURATION IN COMMERCIALLY AVAILABLE OILS

1. Put on safety goggles, gloves, and a lab apron.

2. Use a wax pencil to label five individual test tubes "Peanut oil," "Sunflower oil," "Corn oil," "Cod liver oil," and "Coconut oil."

3. Using a graduated cylinder, measure 10 mL of peanut oil and pour it into the appropriately labeled test tube. Set the test tube in a test-tube rack. Do the same for each of the other four oils.

4. Add two drops of tincture of iodine to each labeled test tube. *Carefully* swirl each test tube to disperse the iodine into small droplets. Return the test tube to the test-tube rack.

5. Let each mixture of oil and iodine stand for at least 10 minutes. Note the time it takes for any color change to occur *after* adding the iodine. Record both the time and color change in **Table 1.**

6. Determine an "unsaturation ranking" for this set of oil samples based on whether a color change occurs (red violet to colorless). If a color change occurs, record the elapsed time. Record your ranking in **Table 1.**

PART 2–DETERMINING THE MELTING POINT OF FOODSTUFFS AND THE DEGREE OF FATTY ACID SATURATION

7. Use a wax pencil to label six individual beakers "Vegetable shortening," "Butter," "Corn oil," "Margarine," "Soft margarine," and "Chocolate."

8. Measure a *level* tablespoon (5 g) of each soft food sample, and place it in its correspondingly labeled beaker. Use a spatula to help level each soft food sample. Place the piece of chocolate in its beaker.

9. Using **Figure 1** as a guide, prepare a water bath. Place one of the beakers prepared in **step 8** in the water bath. Heat on the hot plate's low setting, so that the temperature of the water gradually increases from room temperature. Monitor the temperature. Record the temperature at which the food sample liquefies completely in **Table 2.** Using beaker tongs, remove the warmed sample from the water bath. Repeat for each food sample. Record the room temperature for corn oil.

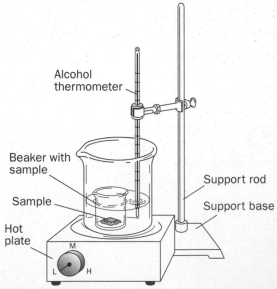

Alcohol thermometer

Beaker with sample

Sample

Hot plate

Support rod

Support base

Figure 1

Name _____ Class _____ Date _____

All Fats Are Not Equal *continued*

10. For each sample tested, review the fatty acid ingredients listed in **Table 2** and your melting-point data. Then rank each food sample from highest saturated fatty acid content to lowest saturated fatty acid content. Record this ranking in **Table 2**.

11. Clean all apparatus and your lab station. Return equipment to its proper place. Dispose of your materials according to your teacher's directions. Dispose of chemicals and waste oils in containers designated by your teacher. Do not pour any chemicals or oils down the drain or put them in the trash unless your teacher directs you to do so. Wash your hands thoroughly after all work is finished and before you leave the lab.

TABLE 1 DETERMINING THE DEGREE OF UNSATURATION IN OILS

Oil type	Number of iodine (I_2) drops	Time to change color (min)	Color change ($\surd$)	Analysis ranking (most unsaturated to least) 1–5
Peanut oil	2		√	4
Sunflower oil	2		√	2
Corn oil	2		√	3
Cod liver oil	2	**Fastest**	√	1
Coconut oil	2	**No change**	√	5

TABLE 2 MELTING POINT AND DEGREE OF SATURATION

Food sample	Melting point (°C)	Fatty acid ingredient(s)	Analysis ranking (most unsaturated to least)
Vegetable shortening	22–32	Hydrogenated and partially hydrogenated vegetable oils	5
Butter	**About 15**	Palmitic acid (29%), oleic acid (27%)	1
Stick margarine	**>soft margarine <butter**	Partially hydrogenated vegetable oils	2
Soft margarine	**<stick margarine**	Partially hydrogenated vegetable oils	3
Corn oil	**Room temperature**	Polyunsaturated acids (34%), oleic acid (50%)	6
Chocolate	**About 32**	Palmitic acid (24%), stearic acid (35%), oleic acid (38%)	4

Answers will vary. Margarines should have lower melting points than butter.

Name _____ Class _____ Date _____

All Fats Are Not Equal *continued*

Analysis

1. **Analyzing Data** Examine your entries in **Table 1.** What trend do you observe in vegetable oils regarding unsaturated fatty acid side chains?

   Most vegetable oils are high in unsaturated fatty acids.

2. **Analyzing Data and Applying Concepts** Coconut oil is a major ingredient in many nondairy creamers and other prepared foods. If an individual is trying to reduce saturated fat intake, would a nondairy creamer containing coconut oil be a good choice? Explain.

   No. Cream (butterfat) and coconut oil are both high in saturated fatty acids.

Answer Key

Concept Review: Carbohydrates and Lipids

1. monosaccharide
2. polysaccharide
3. carbohydrate
4. lipid
5. starch
6. disaccharide
7. glycogen
8. cellulose
9. sugar
10. polymer
11. condensation
12. hydrolysis
13. polysaccharide
14. disaccharide
15. monosaccharide
16. polysaccharide
17.

Carbohydrate	Structure	Role
starch	polysaccharide	storing energy
glycogen	polysaccharide	energy storage in animals
cellulose	polysaccharide	structural rigidity
sucrose	disaccharide	table sugar
glucose	monosaccharide	spreads energy via bloodstream
fructose	monosaccharide	sugar found in fruits
lactose	disaccharide	sugar found in milk products
maltose	disaccharide	malt-flavored sugar
chitin	polysaccharide	insect exoskeleton
amylose	polysaccharide	energy storage in plants

18. Carbohydrates are often used by living organisms to store energy. Other carbohydrates provide rigid structure to plants and animals. Glucose is the chemical that the bloodstream uses to carry energy throughout the body. Sugars can join together and break apart. These processes are the main ways that living organisms capture energy.

19. A condensation reaction is one in which two or more molecules join together into a larger molecule, leaving water or another simple molecule as a byproduct.

20. A hydrolysis reaction is one in which water causes a molecule to break down into two smaller molecules.

Concept Review: Proteins

1. amino acid
2. protein
3. peptide
4. disulfide
5. secondary
6. tertiary
7. primary
8. quaternary
9. helix
10. pleated sheet
11. amino acid
12. enzyme
13. active site
14. disulfide
15. substrate
16. denature
17. trypsin
18. Amino acids form proteins through condensation reactions: the $-OH$ group of a carboxylic acid of one amino acid and an $-H$ from a neighboring amino acid are released as the two amino groups join.
19. 1. Disulfide bridges (covalent bonds) between side chains can form a looped protein or bond two separate polypeptides. 2. Ionic bonds can link different points on a protein. 3. A hydrophobic environment attracts other nonpolar molecules or nonpolar segments of the same protein. 4. Hydrogen bond can form to oxygen atoms, especially carboxyl groups.

20. Enzymes speed up metabolic reactions without being permanently changed or destroyed. They can be thought of as a lock and key: only an enzyme of a specific shape can fit the reactants in the reaction that it is speeding up.

Concept Review: Nucleic Acids

1. DNA
2. deoxyribose
3. nucleic acid
4. gene
5. RNA
6. uracil
7. genetic code
8. nitrogenous
9. DNA fingerprints
10. helix
11. PCR
12. clone
13. stem cell
14. recombinant DNA
15. nucleic acid
16. triplet
17. autoradiograph
18. base
19. DNA replicates by unwinding its double helix, providing two strands. Each strand acts as a template for making a new strand. Each base forms a hydrogen bond to its complementary base (A to T, T to A, C to G, G to C). Eventually the two strands of the original become four strands.
20. a. AUG AAA AGC UUC UCA UAA
    b. START lysine, serine, phenylalanine, serine STOP
    c. ATG AAA AGC TTC TCA TAA
21. a. AUG GAA UGU CUA ACA UGA
    b. START glutamic acid, cysteine, leucine, threonine STOP
    c. ATG GAA TGT CTA ACA TGA
22. Cloning is producing an offspring that is genetically identical to a parent using asexual reproduction methods. In animals, scientists take stem cells and culture them artificially so they grow into complete organisms.

Concept Review: Energy in Living Systems

1. carbon
2. ATP
3. photosynthesis
4. chlorophyll
5. respiration
6. cellular
7. exothermic
8. glycolysis
9. Kreb's
10. mechanical
11. transport
12. synthetic
13. Most plants use chlorophyll to capture energy from sunlight. During this process, called photosynthesis, carbon dioxide and water form glucose and oxygen. The plant stores the glucose by forming larger carbohydrates to use as a source of energy as needed.
14. Animals eat plants, which make carbohydrates that animals, too, can use for energy. Once an animal eats a plant, it breaks the plant's large carbohydrates down into simpler carbohydrates, such as glucose. Glucose can be carried throughout the body in the bloodstream.
15. In photosynthesis, carbon dioxide and water form glucose and oxygen. During respiration the opposite reaction occurs: glucose and oxygen form carbon dioxide and water. Photosynthesis takes in energy. Respiration gives off energy.
16. The first stage of cellular respiration includes glycolysis, in which glucose is split into two molecules of pyruvic acid. This stage produces ATP. The second stage also produces ATP. This stage is called the Kreb's cycle. The overall result is the oxidation of pyruvic acid to form carbon dioxide. The two stages together produce 38 ATP per glucose molecule.

Answer Key

Quiz—Section: Carbohydrates and Lipids

1. a	**6.** c
2. c	**7.** c
3. d	**8.** d
4. b	**9.** b
5. a	**10.** c

Quiz—Section: Proteins

1. a	**6.** b
2. c	**7.** d
3. c	**8.** a
4. b	**9.** c
5. d	**10.** d

Quiz—Section: Nucleic Acids

1. b	**6.** b
2. b	**7.** c
3. a	**8.** a
4. b	**9.** b
5. d	**10.** c

Quiz—Section: Energy in Living Systems

1. a	**6.** d
2. b	**7.** c
3. d	**8.** d
4. b	**9.** a
5. a	**10.** b

Chapter Test

1. b	**11.** a
2. a	**12.** c
3. c	**13.** c
4. b	**14.** b
5. c	**15.** b
6. d	**16.** b
7. d	**17.** c
8. c	**18.** d
9. b	**19.** a
10. a	**20.** d

21. Starch is a source of energy from plants. Glycogen stores energy in the human body. Glucose transfers energy to cells. ATP transfers energy within cells.

22. The genes, which are part of the cell's DNA, provide a template to produce RNA. The RNA contains the code that directs the order of amino acids in the protein.

23. Since the DNA sample for fingerprinting is usually too small to analyze, the PCR process is used to multiply the amount of DNA by many orders of magnitude.

24. The properties are affected by the secondary, tertiary and quaternary structures that are based on orientation of the different parts of the chain in relation to one another and held by intramolecular forces.

25. $6CO_2 + 6H_2O \rightarrow C_6H_{12}O_6 + 6O_2$
(hydrolysis reaction)

$C_6H_{12}O_6 + 6O_2 \rightarrow 6CO_2 + 6H_2O$
(condensation reaction)

During photosynthesis (hydrolysis reaction) energy is obtained from the sun and stored in the chemical bonds of glucose. During respiration (condensation reaction) energy form chemical bonds is transferred to ATP and released as heat.
Plants convert sunlight to the chemical energy for their own fuel and that of animals that eat them. This energy is then used by carnivores that eat those animals.

BIOLOGICAL CHEMISTRY

MULTIPLE CHOICE

1. *Carbohydrate* molecules contain atoms of
   a. carbon and water.
   b. carbon, hydrogen, and oxygen.
   c. carbon hydrogen, and nitrogen.
   d. carbon, hydrogen, nitrogen, and oxygen.

   Answer: B   Difficulty: I   Section: 1   Objective: 1

2. What type of biological molecule provides the main source of human food energy?
   a. hydrocarbon   c. carbohydrate
   b. amino acid   d. protein

   Answer: C   Difficulty: I   Section: 1   Objective: 1

3. The monomer of both starch and cellulose is
   a. an amino acid.   c. dextrose.
   b. fructose.   d. glucose.

   Answer: D   Difficulty: I   Section: 1   Objective: 1

4. What is the primary function of glucose in your body?
   a. to give structure to cell walls
   b. to carry energy through the circulatory system to cells
   c. to store energy
   d. as a starting material for cellulose

   Answer: B   Difficulty: I   Section: 1   Objective: 2

5. The breakdown of polysaccharides is a(n) _____ reaction?
   a. exothermic   c. isothermic
   b. endothermic   d. unstable

   Answer: A   Difficulty: I   Section: 1   Objective: 3

6. What are the two carbohydrates produced by plants?
   a. starch and cellulose
   b. glycogen and cellulose
   c. cellulose and protein
   d. glycogen and starch

   Answer: A   Difficulty: I   Section: 1   Objective: 2

7. The part of a fat molecule that allows it to interact with polar molecules is the _____ end.
   a. hydrophobic   c. amino
   b. hydrophilic   d. None of the above

   Answer: B   Difficulty: I   Section: 1   Objective: 4

8. What are the starting materials for plants to produce carbohydrates?
   a. oxygen and water   c. glucose and oxygen
   b. carbon dioxide and water   d. carbon dioxide, water, and nitrogen

   Answer: B   Difficulty: I   Section: 1   Objective: 3

9. What are the characteristic functional groups of the monomers that form proteins?
   a. an amino group and a hydroxyl group
   b. an amino group and a sulfide linkage
   c. hydrogen bonds between units
   d. an amino group and an organic acid group

   Answer: D   Difficulty: I   Section: 2   Objective: 1

10. The reaction of amino acids to form a protein is an example of
    a. hydrolysis.
    c. condensation.
    b. polymerization.
    d. Both (b) and (c)

    Answer: D   Difficulty: I   Section: 2   Objective: 2

11. Which of these compounds is a product of protein synthesis?
    a. glycine
    c. carbon dioxide
    b. water
    d. glutamic acid

    Answer: B   Difficulty: I   Section: 2   Objective: 2

12. Cysteine is unique among amino acids because it
    a. forms several hydrogen bonds with other amino acids.
    b. includes a phosphorus atom in its structure.
    c. contributes to the primary structure of a protein.
    d. can form a disulfide bridge with other cysteine units.

    Answer: D   Difficulty: I   Section: 2   Objective: 3

13. Side chains affect a protein structure by
    a. forming hydrogen bonds.
    b. contributing to folding of the molecule.
    c. forming chemical bonds with other side chains.
    d. All of the above

    Answer: C   Difficulty: I   Section: 2   Objective: 3

14. What aspect of a protein is described as the tertiary structure?
    a. the order of amino acids
    b. the combination of several chains into a larger structure
    c. folding the molecule in sheet and coils
    d. the three dimensional shape of the protein molecule

    Answer: D   Difficulty: I   Section: 2   Objective: 3

15. Peptide bonds determine the _____ structure of a protein.
    a. primary
    c. tertiary
    b. secondary
    d. All of the above

    Answer: A   Difficulty: I   Section: 2   Objective: 3

16. Which part(s) of a protein structure can be affected by denaturing?
    a. primary
    c. peptide bonds
    b. tertiary
    d. all of the above

    Answer: B   Difficulty: I   Section: 2   Objective: 4

17. The active site of an enzyme functions by
    a. forming a permanent bond with a substrate.
    b. isolating a substrate from other molecules.
    c. transferring energy to the substrate molecule.
    d. holding a substrate in a position that favors a particular reaction.

    Answer: D   Difficulty: I   Section: 2   Objective: 4

18. The base sequence –GGCATGCCA– could represent part of a sequence of
    a. DNA.
    c. either DNA or RNA.
    b. RNA.
    d. neither DNA nor RNA.

    Answer: A   Difficulty: I   Section: 3   Objective: 1

19. The base sequence –GGCAAGCCA– could represent part of a sequence of
    a. DNA.
    c. either DNA or RNA.
    b. RNA.
    d. neither DNA nor RNA.

    Answer: C   Difficulty: I   Section: 3   Objective: 1

20. In a DNA molecule, the base sequence of the two strands is
    a. identical.
    b. complementary.
    c. independent.
    d. random.
    Answer: B   Difficulty: I   Section: 3   Objective: 2

21. A gene is a sequence of DNA that holds the code for
    a. self-replication.
    b. the manufacture of a polypeptide.
    c. the manufacture of a carbohydrate.
    d. recombinant technology.
    Answer: B   Difficulty: I   Section: 3   Objective: 2

22. The first step in protein synthesis is
    a. lining up amino acids in sequence.
    b. unwinding of a segment of the DNA molecule.
    c. unwinding of a segment of the RNA molecule.
    d. addition of an amino acid to DNA.
    Answer: B   Difficulty: I   Section: 3   Objective: 2

23. The process used in genetic fingerprinting to multiply the available DNA is
    a. recombinant technology.
    b. cloning.
    c. cell differentiation.
    d. polymerase chain reaction.
    Answer: D   Difficulty: I   Section: 3   Objective: 3

24. What technique is used to make bacteria that produce drugs?
    a. recombinant technology.
    b. cloning.
    c. cell differentiation.
    d. polymerase chain reaction.
    Answer: A   Difficulty: I   Section: 3   Objective: 3

25. The overall photosynthesis reaction is
    a. endothermic and spontaneous.
    b. endothermic and not spontaneous.
    c. exothermic and spontaneous.
    d. exothermic and not spontaneous.
    Answer: B   Difficulty: I   Section: 4   Objective: 1

26. Cellular respiration is a process that occurs in the cells of
    a. plants
    b. animals
    c. both plants and animals.
    d. neither plants nor animals.
    Answer: C   Difficulty: II   Section: 4   Objective: 2

27. For photosynthesis, the Gibbs free energy is
    a. positive.
    b. negative.
    c. constant.
    d. not known.
    Answer: A   Difficulty: I   Section: 4   Objective: 1

28. For cellular respiration, the value of entropy is
    a. positive.
    b. negative.
    c. constant.
    d. not known.
    Answer: A   Difficulty: I   Section: 4   Objective: 2

29. During cellular respiration
    a. ATP is converted to ADP
    b. ADP is converted to ATP
    c. ATP is converted to glucose
    d. ADP is converted to glucose
    Answer: B   Difficulty: I   Section: 4   Objective: 2

COMPLETION

30. Sugars in a polysaccharide are linked together by bonds to a(n) _____ atom.
    Answer: oxygen   Difficulty: I   Section: 1   Objective: 1

31. The plant polysaccharide _____ provides energy to the cells of plants and animals.
    Answer: starch   Difficulty: I   Section: 1   Objective: 2

32. Plants use the polysaccharide _____ for structural strength.
    Answer: cellulose   Difficulty: I   Section: 1   Objective: 2

33. The polysaccharide _____ is manufactured in animal cells to store energy in muscles.
    Answer: glycogen   Difficulty: I   Section: 1   Objective: 2

34. Water is a byproduct of the _____ reaction that builds polysaccharides and a reactant in the
    _____ reaction that breaks them apart.
    Answer: condensation, hydrolysis
    Difficulty: I   Section: 1   Objective: 3

35. The products of the hydrolysis of glycogen are _____ and _____.
    Answer: glucose, water
    Difficulty: I   Section: 1   Objective: 3

36. The reaction that forms polysaccharides also produces molecules of _____.
    Answer: water   Difficulty: I   Section: 1   Objective: 3

37. The letter ____ is used to designate a side chain on an amino acid or protein molecule.
    Answer: R   Difficulty: I   Section: 2   Objective: 1

38. The two groups involved in a peptide bond are the _____ group and the _____
    group.
    Answer: amino, acid   Difficulty: I   Section: 2   Objective: 1

39. A(n) _____ bond is formed by the condensation reaction of two amino acids.
    Answer: peptide   Difficulty: I   Section: 2   Objective: 2

40. In a protein molecule, cysteine side chains can link parts of the molecule using _____.
    Answer: disulfide bonds or bridges
    Difficulty: I   Section: 2   Objective: 3

41. In an enzyme, the _____ is the part of the protein that interacts with a substrate.
    Answer: active site   Difficulty: I   Section: 2   Objective: 4

42. An enzyme and its _____ fit together like a lock and key.
    Answer: substrate   Difficulty: I   Section: 2   Objective: 4

43. Several distinct polypeptide chains together form the _____ structure of some proteins.
    Answer: quaternary   Difficulty: I   Section: 2   Objective: 3

44. An organism's _____ store all of its genetic information.
    Answer: nucleic acids or DNA
    Difficulty: I   Section: 3   Objective:1

45. Nucleic acids are built from units consisting of three parts: a(n) _____, a(n) _____,
    and a(n) _____.
    Answer: sugar, phosphate group, nitrogenous base
    Difficulty: I   Section: 3   Objective: 1

46. The sugar molecule _____ is part of a DNA nucleotide.
    Answer: deoxyribose   Difficulty: I   Section: 3   Objective: 1

47. DNA genetic information is translated into an amino acid sequence by _____.
    Answer: RNA   Difficulty: I   Section: 3   Objective: 2

48. The sequence –UUUCCCCGAAACGAC– provides the code for _____ amino acids.
    Answer: five   Difficulty: I   Section: 3   Objective: 2

49. Scientist use _____ to insert the genes from one organism into the cells of another organism.
    Answer: recombinant DNA technology
    Difficulty: I   Section: 3   Objective: 3

50. The shape of a DNA molecule is described as a(n) _____.
    Answer: double helix   Difficulty: I   Section: 3   Objective: 3

51. Using the technique of _____, an organism can be identified by a sample of its DNA.
    Answer: DNA fingerprinting
    Difficulty: I   Section: 3   Objective: 3

52. The products of photosynthesis are _____ and _____.
    Answer: glucose, oxygen
    Difficulty: I   Section: 4   Objective: 1

53. The source of energy to drive the reaction $6H_2O + 6CO_2 \rightarrow C_6H_{12}O_6 + 6O_2$ is _____.
    Answer: sunlight   Difficulty: I   Section: 4   Objective: 2

54. During _____, the first stage of cellular respiration, the molecule _____ is broken down.
    Answer: glycolysis, glucose
    Difficulty: I   Section: 4   Objective: 2

55. The overall reaction of cellular respiration produces _____ molecules of ATP.
    Answer : 38   Difficulty: I   Section: 4   Objective: 2

56. The molecule that provides readily available energy to cells is _____, abbreviated as _____.
    Answer: adenosine triphosphate, ATP
    Difficulty: I   Section: 4   Objective: 2

57. The structures of ATP and ADP differ by a _____.
    Answer: phosphate group
    Difficulty: I   Section: 4   Objective: 2

58. There are three types of work, _____, _____, and _____, that are fueled by ATP in cells.
    Answer: synthetic, mechanical, transport
    Difficulty: I   Section: 4   Objective: 2

59. Because the cellular respiration reactions are less than 100% efficient, the process also gives off energy as _____.
    Answer: heat   Difficulty: I   Section: 4   Objective: 2

SHORT ANSWER

60. How do the structures of cellulose and starch differ?
    Answer: The glucose units are oriented differently around the carbon-oxygen bonds.
    Difficulty: I   Section: 1   Objective: 1

61. How is the formation of biological polymers different from most industrial polymerization processes?

    Answer: Biological polymers are formed at much lower temperatures than most industrial processes. In addition, most industrial polymerizations are not carried out in solution.

    Difficulty: II   Section: 1   Objective: 2

62. Describe a biological role of cellulose, of starch and of glycogen.

    Answer: Cellulose provides structural strength to plants; starch stores plant energy used by plants and animals; glycogen stores energy in animal muscles.

    Difficulty: I   Section: 1   Objective: 2

63. Describe the reaction that breaks polysaccharides into smaller molecules. What is this reaction called?

    Answer: The reaction that breaks polysaccharides into smaller molecules is one in which a water molecule is used and is called a hydrolysis reaction. A hydrogen atom is added to the oxygen on one sugar and a hydroxyl group is added to the other sugar.

    Difficulty: II   Section: 1   Objective: 3

64. What roles do lipids play in living systems?

    Answer: Lipids are used in animals for energy storage as fats, cell membranes are made of phospholipids, steroids are used for chemical signaling.

    Difficulty: I   Section: 1   Objective: 4

65. Draw a structural diagram of an amino acid and label the key functional groups.

    Answer: The structure must show a central carbon atom joined to a hydrogen atom, an R side chain, an amino group, $-NH_2$, and a carboxylic acid group, $-COOH$.

    Difficulty: I   Section: 2   Objective: 1

66. What is a peptide bond and what is the reaction that forms it?

    Answer: A peptide bond is the chemical bond between the acid group of one amino acid and the base group of another. It is formed by a condensation reaction that yields a molecule of water.

    Difficulty: II   Section: 2   Objective:2

67. Describe the primary, secondary, tertiary, and quaternary structures of a protein.

    Answer: Primary structure is the order of amino acids in the chain. Secondary structure is the arrangement of portions of the molecule into sheets and helices. Tertiary structure is the three-dimensional arrangement of the molecule. Quaternary structure is the combination of several polypeptide chains by intermolecular forces to form one protein.

    Difficulty: I   Section: 2   Objective: 3

68. How do side chains on amino acids contribute to protein structure?

    Answer: The side chains form hydrogen bonds, chemical bonds, and other intramolecular interactions that cause the three-dimensional structure of the protein.

    Difficulty: I   Section: 2   Objective: 3

69. What is the effect of denaturing on protein structure?

    Answer: When a protein is denatured, it retains the same primary structure but the higher structural elements are changed, causing the protein to have a different shape.

    Difficulty: II   Section: 2   Objective: 4

70. Why is it necessary for a gene to use three base pairs to code each amino acid?

    Answer: Because there are twenty different amino acids. Since there are four different base combinations, two pairs could only code $4 \times 4 = 16$ different combinations.

    Difficulty: II   Section: 3   Objective: 1

71. Describe the process by which a gene codes the synthesis of a protein.

    Answer: The helixes of the DNA molecule separate at the gene, coding a sequence of RNA. Triplets of bases on the RNA direct the order of amino acids in the protein.

    Difficulty: II   Section: 3   Objective: 2

72. A tiny drop of blood can provide DNA for DNA fingerprinting, although the analysis requires much more material than the blood sample provides. How does the analyst obtain enough DNA for the test?

    Answer: The polymerase chain reaction (PCR) technique replicates a segment of DNA in a reaction that can be repeated to multiply the amount of material by a factor of a million or more.

    Difficulty: II   Section: 3   Objective:3

73. How do the structures of DNA and RNA differ?

    Answer: The two compounds have a different sugar molecule in the nucleotides, deoxyribose for DNA and ribose for RNA. In RNA, the base uracil replaces the base thymine of a DNA strand.

    Difficulty: I   Section: 3   Objective: 1

74. Many reactions in cells that are not spontaneous occur constantly in your body. How do these reactions occur, if they are not thermodynamically favored?

    Answer: The reactions are coupled to the hydrolysis of ATP to ADP, which is spontaneous and exothermic, providing energy to drive other reactions.

    Difficulty: II   Section: 4   Objective: 2

75. Is the entropy change associated with photosynthesis positive or negative? Is the entropy change associated with respiration positive or negative?

    Answer: The entropy change for photosynthesis is negative, and the entropy change for respiration is positive.

    Difficulty: III   Section: 4   Objective: 1

PROBLEMS

RNA triplet	Amino acid
UUC	phenylalanine
CUU	leucine
AAU	asparagine
GGU	glycine
AAA	lysine

76. What is the polypeptide specified by the RNA sequence: –AAAAAUCUUCUUUUCGGUAAUAAAAAU–?

    Answer: lysine-asparagine-leucine-leucine-phenylalanine-glycine-asparagine-lysine-asparagine

    Difficulty: II   Section: 2   Objective: 3

77. What is the polypeptide specified by the DNA sequence: –TTTAAGGAAAAGCCATTT–?

    Answer: lysine-phenylalanine-leucine-phenylalanine-glycine-lysine

    Difficulty: III   Section: 2   Objective: 3

ESSAY QUESTIONS

78. Explain how photosynthesis and respiration are complementary reactions. What is the energy flow of these reactions?

    Answer: Photosynthesis is the process of building glucose molecules from carbon dioxide and water, while respiration is the process of breaking glucose down into carbon dioxide and water. Energy flows into the process as sunlight during photosynthesis and is released during respiration.

    Difficulty: II   Section: 1   Objective: 3

79. Why are enzymes essential to life? Why are enzymes classified as catalysts?

    Answer: Enzymes help many reactions in cells that might not otherwise occur or would proceed too slowly by bringing substrates together and positioning them properly for reaction. Enzymes are catalysts because they promote the reaction without being consumed.

    Difficulty: II   Section: 2   Objective: 4

80. What are some potential advantages and disadvantages of recombinant DNA technology?

    Answer: The advantages are the ability to cause cells to produce biological molecules that are useful as medicines or to protect plants against pests. The disadvantages include the possibility of constructing organisms that could be unexpectedly harmful or that could escape into the environment without natural controls.

    Difficulty: II   Section: 3   Objective: 3

81. Even though some animals are completely carnivorous, eating only other animals, their energy actually comes from the sun. Explain.

    Answer: Even though carnivores eat only other animals, their prey either obtains energy from plants or from other animals that eat plants. Ultimately the source of all energy for plant and animal cell functions is the energy stored in carbohydrates during photosynthesis.

    Difficulty: II   Section: 4   Objective: 2